THIS BOOK BELONGS TO:

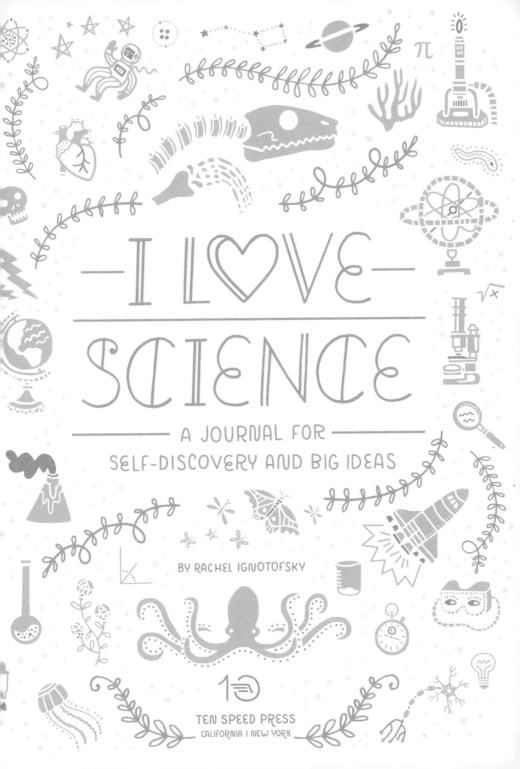

I ♥ LOVE

SCIENCE

A JOURNAL FOR
SELF-DISCOVERY AND BIG IDEAS

BY RACHEL IGNOTOFSKY

TEN SPEED PRESS
CALIFORNIA I NEW YORK

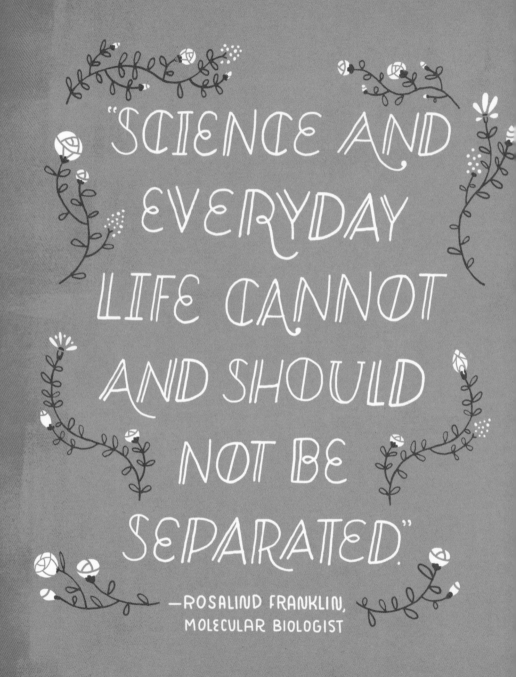

"SCIENCE AND EVERYDAY LIFE CANNOT AND SHOULD NOT BE SEPARATED."

—ROSALIND FRANKLIN,
MOLECULAR BIOLOGIST

ABOUT THIS JOURNAL

DO YOU WAKE UP EVERY DAY WITH CURIOSITY AND AN EXCITEMENT TO LEARN MORE ABOUT THE WORLD? IF SO, THEN THIS JOURNAL IS FOR YOU!

USE THESE PAGES TO WRITE DOWN YOUR BIG IDEAS, ASK YOUR QUESTIONS ABOUT THE UNIVERSE, AND DREAM AND SCHEME ABOUT HOW TO FOLLOW YOUR PASSIONS, WHEREVER THEY TAKE YOU. THERE ARE ALSO SOME HANDY REFERENCE PAGES IN THE FRONT WITH ALL SORTS OF INFORMATION YOU MIGHT NEED AS YOU EXPERIMENT.

HAPPY JOURNALING!

THE SCIENTIFIC METHOD

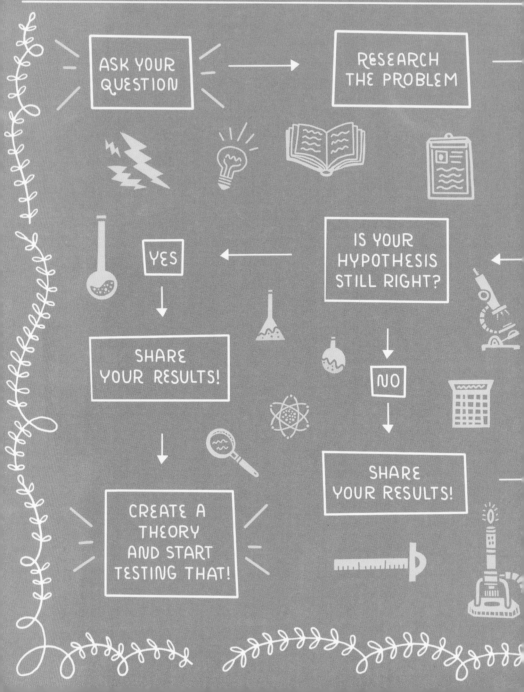

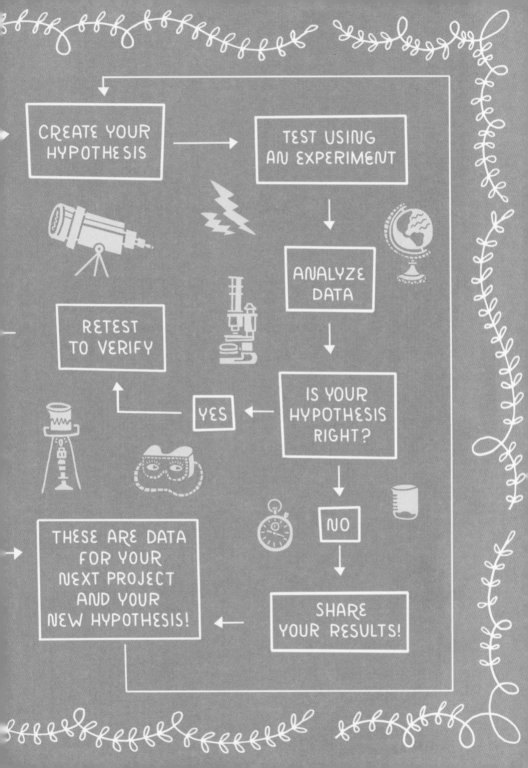

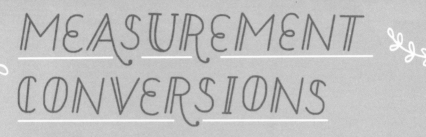

MEASUREMENT CONVERSIONS

CAPACITY

16 OUNCES = 1 PINT

2 CUPS = 1 PINT

2 PINTS = 1 QUART

4 QUARTS = 1 GALLON

10 mL = 1 cL

100 cL = 1 L

100 L = 1 hl

1 QUART = 0.94635 L

1.0567 QUART = 1 L

1 GALLON = 3.7854 L

0.2642 GALLON = 1 L

VOLUME

$1,728 \text{ INCHES}^3 = 1 \text{ FOOT}^3$

$27 \text{ FEET}^3 = 1 \text{ YARD}^3$

$1,000 \text{ mm}^3 = 1 \text{ cm}^3$

$1,000 \text{ cm}^3 = 1 \text{ dm}^3$

$1,000 \text{ dm}^3 = 1 \text{ m}^3$

$1 \text{ INCH}^3 = 16.387 \text{ cm}^3$

$0.0610 \text{ INCHES}^3 = 1 \text{ cm}^3$

$1 \text{ YARD}^3 = 0.7646 \text{ m}^3$

$1.3080 \text{ YARD}^3 = 1 \text{ m}^3$

LENGTH

12 INCHES = 1 FOOT

3 FEET = 1 YARD

220 YARDS = 1 FURLONG

5,280 FEET = 1 SM

6,076.1 FEET = 1 nM

10 mm = 1 cm

10 cm = 1 dm

10 dm = 1 m

10 m = 1 dam

1,000 m = 1 km

1 INCH = 2.54 cm

0.3937 INCH = 1 cm

1 SM = 1.6093 Km

0.6214 SM = 1 Km

1 nM = 1.8519 Km

0.5400 nM = 1 Km

AREA

$144 \text{ INCH}^2 = 1 \text{ FOOT}^2$

$9 \text{ FEET}^2 = 1 \text{ YARD}^2$

$4,840 \text{ YARDS}^2 = 1 \text{ ACRE}$

$640 \text{ ACRES} = 1 \text{ MILE}^2$

$100 \text{ mm}^2 = 1 \text{ cm}^2$

$100 \text{ cm}^2 = 1 \text{ dm}^2$

$10,000 \text{ cm}^2 = 1 \text{ m}^2$

$100 \text{ m}^2 = 1 \text{ dam}^2$

$100 \text{ dam}^2 = 1 \text{ ha}$

$10,000 \text{ dam}^2 = 1 \text{ Km}^2$

$1 \text{ INCH}^2 = 6.4516 \text{ cm}^2$

$0.155 \text{ INCH}^2 = 1 \text{ cm}^2$

$1 \text{ ACRE} = 0.4047 \text{ ha}$

$2.471 \text{ ACRES} = 1 \text{ ha}$

$1 \text{ SM}^2 = 2.5900 \text{ Km}^2$

$0.3861 \text{ SM}^2 = 1 \text{ Km}^2$

GEOMETRY FORMULAS

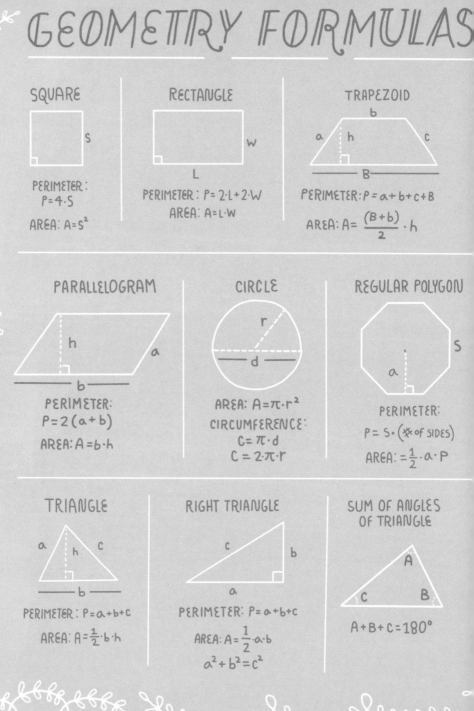

SQUARE

s

PERIMETER:
$P = 4 \cdot S$

AREA: $A = S^2$

RECTANGLE

W

L

PERIMETER: $P = 2 \cdot L + 2 \cdot W$

AREA: $A = L \cdot W$

TRAPEZOID

b

a   h   c

B

PERIMETER: $P = a + b + c + B$

AREA: $A = \dfrac{(B + b)}{2} \cdot h$

PARALLELOGRAM

h

a

b

PERIMETER:
$P = 2(a + b)$

AREA: $A = b \cdot h$

CIRCLE

r

d

AREA: $A = \pi \cdot r^2$

CIRCUMFERENCE:
$C = \pi \cdot d$
$C = 2 \cdot \pi \cdot r$

REGULAR POLYGON

S

a

PERIMETER:
$P = S \cdot (\text{\# of SIDES})$

AREA: $= \dfrac{1}{2} \cdot a \cdot P$

TRIANGLE

a   h   c

b

PERIMETER: $P = a + b + c$

AREA: $A = \dfrac{1}{2} \cdot b \cdot h$

RIGHT TRIANGLE

c   b

a

PERIMETER: $P = a + b + c$

AREA: $A = \dfrac{1}{2} \cdot a \cdot b$

$a^2 + b^2 = c^2$

SUM OF ANGLES OF TRIANGLE

A

c   B

$A + B + C = 180°$

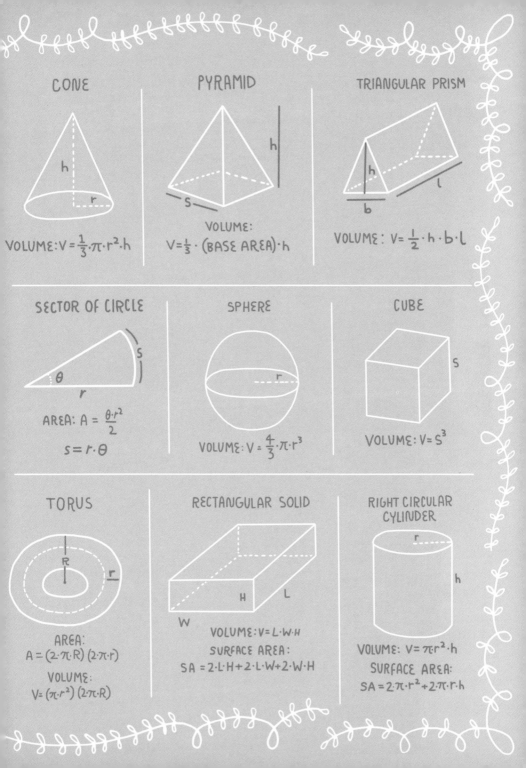

CONE

VOLUME: $V = \frac{1}{3} \cdot \pi \cdot r^2 \cdot h$

PYRAMID

VOLUME:
$V = \frac{1}{3} \cdot (\text{BASE AREA}) \cdot h$

TRIANGULAR PRISM

VOLUME: $V = \frac{1}{2} \cdot h \cdot b \cdot l$

SECTOR OF CIRCLE

AREA: $A = \frac{\theta \cdot r^2}{2}$

$s = r \cdot \theta$

SPHERE

VOLUME: $V = \frac{4}{3} \cdot \pi \cdot r^3$

CUBE

VOLUME: $V = S^3$

TORUS

AREA:
$A = (2 \cdot \pi \cdot R)(2 \cdot \pi \cdot r)$

VOLUME:
$V = (\pi \cdot r^2)(2 \pi \cdot R)$

RECTANGULAR SOLID

VOLUME: $V = L \cdot W \cdot H$
SURFACE AREA:
$SA = 2 \cdot L \cdot H + 2 \cdot L \cdot W + 2 \cdot W \cdot H$

RIGHT CIRCULAR CYLINDER

VOLUME: $V = \pi r^2 \cdot h$
SURFACE AREA:
$SA = 2 \cdot \pi \cdot r^2 + 2 \cdot \pi \cdot r \cdot h$

PHYSICS EQUATIONS

NEWTON'S LAWS

$$a = \frac{F_{unb}}{m}$$

$$W = mg = F_g$$

$$\mu = \frac{F_f}{F_N}$$

$$F_g = \frac{Gm_1 m_2}{r^2}$$

ENERGY AND POWER

$$W = Fd$$

$$P = \frac{W}{t}$$

$$W = \Delta KE = -\Delta PE$$

$$E_k = \frac{1}{2}mv^2$$

$$E_p = mgh$$

$$\% eff = \frac{ENERGY\ OUTPUT}{ENERGY\ INPUT} \times 100\%$$

ACCELERATION

$$\bar{a} = \frac{\Delta v}{\Delta t}$$

$$a = \frac{dv}{dt}$$

MOMENTUM

$$P = mv$$

$$P_f = P_i + I$$

VELOCITY DISTANCE AND TIME

TRIGONOMETRY

$$a^2 + b^2 = c^2$$

$$\sin\theta = \frac{opp}{hyp}$$

$$\cos\theta = \frac{adj}{hyp}$$

$$\tan\theta = \frac{opp}{adj}$$

$$area = \frac{1}{2}ab$$

CONSTANT VELOCITY

$$v = \frac{\Delta d}{\Delta t} = \frac{d_f - d_i}{t_f - t_i}$$

SPECIAL RELATIVITY

$$t = \frac{t_0}{\sqrt{1 - \frac{v^2}{c^2}}}$$

$$E = mc^2$$

WAVE MOTION AND OPTICS

$$v = f\lambda$$

$$T = \frac{1}{f}$$

$$\frac{1}{d_o} + \frac{1}{d_i} = \frac{1}{f}$$

$$m = -\frac{d_i}{d_o}$$

$$\theta_c = \sin^{-1}\left(\frac{n_2}{n_1}\right)$$

QUADRATIC FORMULA

If: $ax^2 + bx + c = 0$

THEN: $x = \dfrac{-b \pm \sqrt{b^2 - 4ac}}{2a}$

CONSTANT ACCELERATION

$$d = \frac{1}{2}at^2$$

$$d = v_i t + \frac{1}{2}at^2$$

$$d = \left(\frac{v_i + v_f}{2}\right)t$$

$$v_f = v_i + at$$

$$v_f^2 = v_i^2 + 2ad$$

$$v_{av} = \frac{v_i + v_f}{2} = \frac{d_f - d_i}{t_f - t_i}$$

$$a = \frac{\Delta v}{\Delta t} = \frac{v_f - v_i}{t_f - t_i}$$

CONSTANTS

$$g = 9.8 \text{ m/s}^2$$

$$c = 3.00 \cdot 10^8 \text{ m/s}$$

$$G = 6.67 \cdot 10^{-11} \text{ Nm}^2/\text{kg}^2$$

$$\pi \approx 3.14$$

PERCENT ERROR

% DIFF = DIFF/AVERAGE · 100%

% ERROR = DIFF/TRUE · 100%

PERIODIC TABLE
OF ELEMENTS

GROUP→

PERIOD

Group	1	2	3	4	5	6	7	8
1	1 H							
2	3 Li	4 Be						
3	11 Na	12 Mg						
4	19 K	20 Ca	21 Sc	22 Ti	23 V	24 Cr	25 Mn	26 Fe
5	37 Rb	38 Sr	39 Y	40 Zr	41 Nb	42 Mo	43 Tc	44 Ru
6	55 Cs	56 Ba	* 57-71	72 Hf	73 Ta	74 W	75 Re	76 Os
7	87 Fr	88 Ra	** 89-103	104 Rf	105 Db	106 Sg	107 Bh	108 Hs

ATOMIC NU
(EQUAL TO TH

SYMBOL

6
C

*		57 La	58 Ce	59 Pr	60 Nd	61 Pm	62 Sm
**		89 Ac	90 Th	91 Pa	92 U	93 Np	94 Pu

10	11	12	13	14	15	16	17	18
								2 He
F PROTONS)			5 B	6 C	7 N	8 O	9 F	10 Ne
			13 Al	14 Si	15 P	16 S	17 Cl	18 Ar
28 Ni	29 Cu	30 Zn	31 Ga	32 Ge	33 As	34 Se	35 Br	36 Kr
46 Pd	47 Ag	48 Cd	49 In	50 Sn	51 Sb	52 Te	53 I	54 Xe
78 Pt	79 Au	80 Hg	81 Tl	82 Pb	83 Bi	84 Po	85 At	86 Rn
110 Ds	111 Rg	112 Cn	113 Uut	114 Fl	115 Uup	116 Lv	117 Uus	118 Uuo

64 Gd	65 Tb	66 Dy	67 Ho	68 Er	69 Tm	70 Yb	71 Lu
96 Cm	97 Bk	98 Cf	99 Es	100 Fm	101 Md	102 No	103 Lr

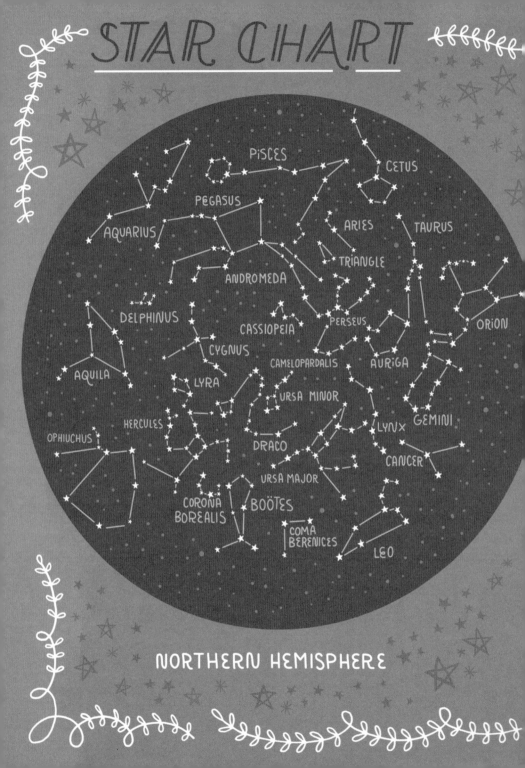

STAR CHART

PISCES
CETUS
PEGASUS
AQUARIUS
ARIES
TAURUS
TRIANGLE
ANDROMEDA
DELPHINUS
PERSEUS
ORION
CASSIOPEIA
CYGNUS
CAMELOPARDALIS
AURIGA
AQUILA
LYRA
URSA MINOR
GEMINI
HERCULES
LYNX
OPHIUCHUS
DRACO
CANCER
URSA MAJOR
CORONA
BOREALIS
BOÖTES
COMA
BERENICES
LEO

NORTHERN HEMISPHERE

SOUTHERN HEMISPHERE

HTML CODE VOCABULARY

HTML WEBSITE STRUCTURE

```
<html>
<head>
<title>Website Name</title>
</head>
<body>
website content & info...
</body>
</html>
```

TEXT

`<pre></pre>` - PREFORMATTED TEXT

`<h?></h?>` "?" = 1-6 BIG-SMALL HEADLINE

`<b></b>` - BOLD TEXT

`<i></i>` - ITALIC TEXT

`<tt></tt>` - TYPEWRITER-STYLE TEXT

`<cite></cite>` - CITATION

`<font size="?"></font>` - SIZE OF FONT

`<font color="??????"></font>` - COLOR

FORMATTING

`<p></p>` - NEW PARAGRAPH

`<p align="?">` - TEXT ALLIGNMENT
(LEFT, RIGHT, OR CENTER)

`<br>` - INSERTS A LINE BREAK

LISTS

`<dl></dl>` - DEFINITION LIST

`<dt>` - COMES BEFORE DEFINITION TERMS

`<dd>` - COMES BEFORE DEFINITIONS

`<ol></ol>` - DEFINE ORDERED LIST

`<ul></ul>` - DEFINE UNORDERED LIST

`<li></li>` - ELEMENTS FOR LIST ITEM

LINKS

`<a href="URL"></a>` - LINK

`<a href="mailto:EMAIL"></a>` - EMAIL

`<a href="URL"><img src="URL"></a>` - IMAGE LINK

`<a name="?"></a>` - TARGET LOCATION

`<a href="*?"></a>` - LINK TO A TARGET LOCATION

TABLE

table border="?"> - BORDER WIDTH AROUND CELLS

table cellspacing="?"> - SPACE BETWEEN TABLE CELLS

table cellpadding="?"> - CELL PADDING

table width="?"> - WIDTH OF TABLE

tr align="?"> - CELL ALIGNMENT (LEFT, RIGHT, OR CENTER)

tr valign="?"> - VERTICAL ALIGNMENT (TOP, MIDDLE, OR BOTTOM)

td colspan="?"> - NUMBER OF COLUMNS

td rowspan="?"> - NUMBER OF ROWS

FRAMES

frameset>...</frameset> - FRAMESET

frameset rows="?,?"> - NUMBER OF ROWS

frameset cols="?,?"> - NUMBER OF COLUMNS

noframes></noframes> - FOR BROWSERS THAT DON'T SUPPORT FRAMES

IMAGES

<img src="URL" - BASIC IMAGE

img src="NAME"align="?"> - ALIGNMENT

lt="TEXT..." - ALTERNATE TEXT

width="?" - IMAGE WIDTH

height="?" - IMAGE HEIGHT

FORMS

<form></form>

<select multiple name="?"size="?"></select> - SCROLLING MENU & AMOUNT OF ITEMS

<option> - SETS OFF EACH MENU ITEM

<select name="?"></selct> - PULLDOWN MENU

<textarea name="?"cols="?" rows="?"></textarea name> - TEXT BOX AREA WIDTH AND HEIGHT

<input type="checkbox"name="?"> - CHECKBOX & TEXT TAGS

<input type="radio"name="?"value="?"> - RADIO BUTTON

<input type="text..." name="?" size="?"> - TEXT AREA & CHARACTER LENGTH

<input type="submit"value="?"> - DEFINES SUBMIT BUTTON

<button type="submit">Submit</button> - CREATES SUBMIT BUTTON

<input type="reset"> - CREATES A RESET BUTTON

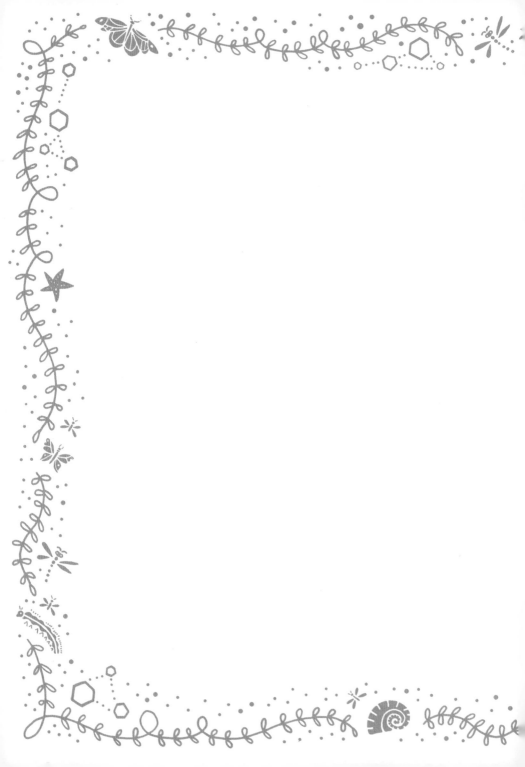

"I HAVE FOUR TIPS: 1. CURIOSITY. GO AFTER YOUR CURIOSITY. 2. MORE CURIOSITY. 3. EVEN MORE CURIOSITY. 4. PASSION. IT'S NOT ENOUGH TO BE CURIOUS—ONE HAS TO REALLY LOVE WHAT ONE DOES."
—ADA YONATH, NOBEL PRIZE–WINNING CRYSTALLOGRAPHER

HOW DO YOU USE WHAT YOU KNOW ABOUT SCIENCE OR MATH IN YOUR EVERYDAY LIFE?

_____

_____

_____

_____

_____

_____

_____

_____

_____

_____

_____

_____

_____

_____

_____

_____

_____

_____

_____

"THERE IS NO JOY MORE INTENSE THAN THAT OF
COMING UPON A FACT THAT CANNOT BE UNDERSTOOD
IN TERMS OF CURRENTLY ACCEPTED IDEAS."
—CECILIA PAYNE-GAPOSCHKIN, ASTRONOMER AND ASTROPHYSICIST

NAME A TIME WHEN YOU'VE HAD TO COME UP WITH A
SOLUTION TO A DIFFICULT PROBLEM. WHAT WAS THE
SOLUTION AND HOW DID YOU FIGURE IT OUT?

"I WAS TAUGHT THAT THE WAY OF PROGRESS IS NEITHER SWIFT NOR EASY."

—MARIE CURIE,
NOBEL PRIZE-WINNING
PHYSICIST AND CHEMIST

WHAT BIG GOAL DO YOU WANT TO ACCOMPLISH THIS YEAR? WHAT WILL YOU DO THIS MONTH TO HELP ACHIEVE THAT GOAL? WHAT WILL YOU DO THIS WEEK TO HELP ACHIEVE THAT GOAL?

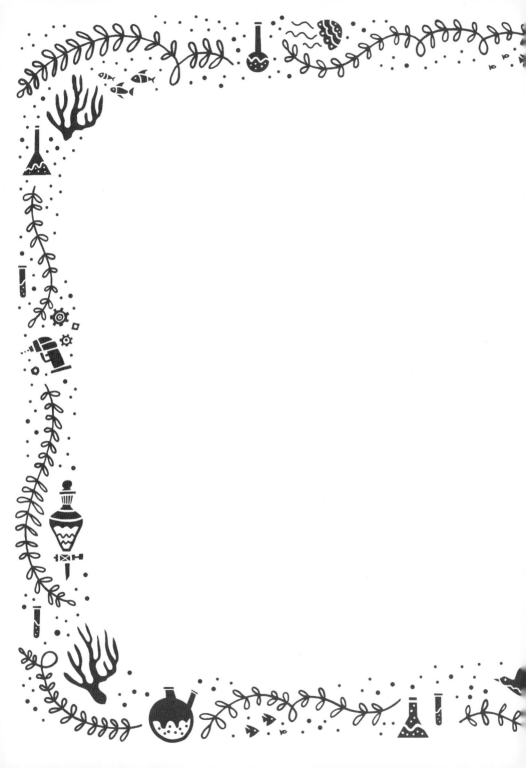

"WHEN YOU REALIZE THE VALUE OF ALL LIFE, YOU DWELL LESS ON WHAT IS PAST AND CONCENTRATE MORE ON THE PRESERVATION OF THE FUTURE."
—DIAN FOSSEY, ZOOLOGIST, PRIMATOLOGIST, AND ANTHROPOLOGIST

WHAT ARE YOUR FAVORITE ANIMALS? WHY?

_____
_____
_____
_____
_____
_____
_____
_____
_____
_____
_____
_____
_____
_____
_____
_____
_____
_____
_____
_____
_____
_____

"DON'T LET ANYONE ROB YOU OF YOUR IMAGINATION,
YOUR CREATIVITY, OR YOUR CURIOSITY. IT'S YOUR
PLACE IN THE WORLD; IT'S YOUR LIFE."
—MAE JEMISON, ASTRONAUT, EDUCATOR, DOCTOR,
AND FIRST AFRICAN–AMERICAN WOMAN IN SPACE

FIND A UNIQUE OBJECT IN NATURE
AND OBSERVE IT CLOSELY. DRAW WHAT YOU SEE.

DETAILED OBSERVATIONS

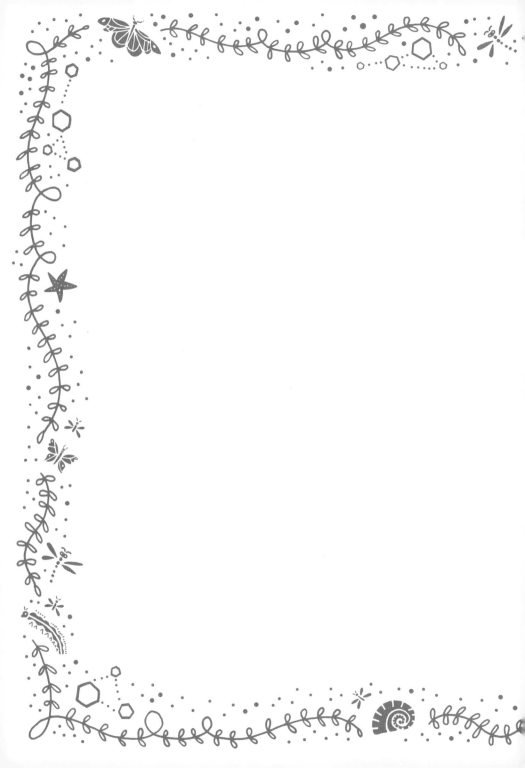

"ALL SORTS OF THINGS CAN HAPPEN WHEN YOU'RE OPEN
TO NEW IDEAS AND PLAYING AROUND WITH THINGS."
—STEPHANIE K. WOLEK, CHEMIST

IF YOU COULD HAVE ONE SUPERPOWER,
WHAT WOULD IT BE AND WHY?

_____

_____

_____

_____

_____

_____

_____

_____

_____

_____

_____

_____

_____

_____

_____

_____

_____

_____

_____

_____

_____

"I HADN'T BEEN AWARE THAT THERE WERE DOORS CLOSED
TO ME UNTIL I STARTED KNOCKING ON THEM."
—GERTRUDE ELION, PHARMACOLOGIST
AND NOBEL PRIZE–WINNING BIOCHEMIST

HAVE YOU EVER HAD TO BREAK THE
RULES TO DO THE RIGHT THING?

"LIVE WITH INTEGRITY AND LET YOUR CONSCIENCE BE YOUR GUIDE. BE A PIONEER AND FOLLOW YOUR HEART, CONTRIBUTING TO FUTURE HUMANKIND."

— SAU LAN WU, PARTICLE PHYSICIST

WHAT HAVE YOU ACHIEVED THAT YOU ARE MOST PROUD OF?

"MOST ENGINEERS LIKE TO PROCEED FROM 'A' TO 'B' TO 'C' IN A SERIES OF LOGICAL STEPS. I'M THE RARE ENGINEER WHO SAYS THE ANSWER IS OBVIOUSLY 'Z'."
—SOPHIE WILSON, COMPUTER SCIENTIST AND SOFTWARE ENGINEER

WHAT NEW TECHNOLOGY DO YOU THINK SHOULD BE INVENTED? WHAT PROBLEMS WOULD IT SOLVE?

_____

_____

_____

_____

_____

_____

_____

_____

_____

_____

_____

_____

_____

_____

_____

_____

_____

"WE HAVE A HUNGER OF THE MIND WHICH ASKS
FOR KNOWLEDGE OF ALL AROUND US, AND THE MORE
WE GAIN, THE MORE IS OUR DESIRE; THE MORE WE
SEE, THE MORE WE ARE CAPABLE OF SEEING."
—MARIA MITCHELL, ASTRONOMER

IF YOU COULD GO BACK IN TIME, WHERE AND WHEN
WOULD YOU GO? WHO WOULD YOU TALK TO AND WHY?

"THE SMARTER YOU ARE, THE BETTER PREPARED YOU ARE TO MAKE DECISIONS IN YOUR LIFE, THE MORE LIKELY YOU ARE TO LEAD A SATISFYING LIFE AND BE GLAMOROUS AND FUN AND ANYTHING YOU WANT TO BE."
—DANICA MCKELLAR, MATHEMATICIAN, AUTHOR, AND ACTOR

WHAT NATURAL PHENOMENA WOULD
YOU LIKE TO WITNESS AND WHY?

"DON'T BE AFRAID TO ASK PEOPLE FOR
HELP—AND THEN FEEL FREE TO IGNORE IT!"
—ELIZABETH BLACKBURN, NOBEL PRIZE-WINNING MOLECULAR BIOLOGIST

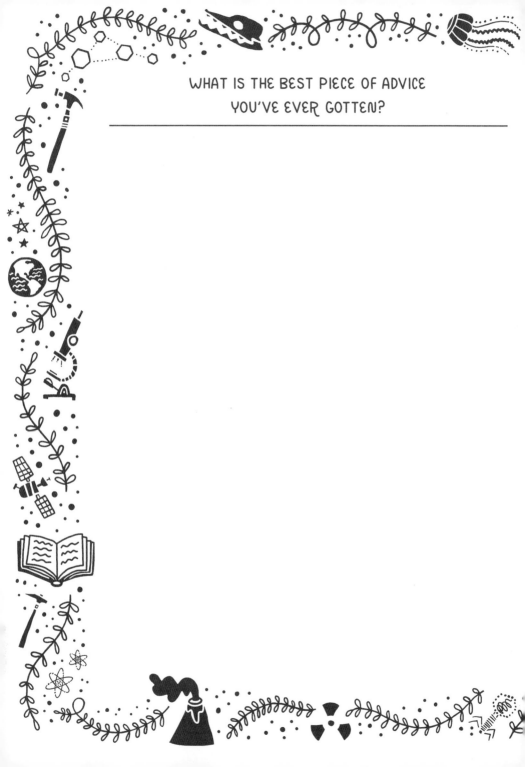

WHAT IS THE BEST PIECE OF ADVICE
YOU'VE EVER GOTTEN?

"YOU CAN CHANGE THE WORLD, FOR YOU ARE MADE OF STAR STUFF, AND YOU ARE CONNECTED TO THE UNIVERSE."

—VERA RUBIN, ASTRONOMER

WHAT ARE SOME BIG DREAMS
YOU HAVE FOR YOUR FUTURE?

"MANY OF US ASK WHAT CAN I, AS ONE PERSON, DO, BUT HISTORY SHOWS US THAT EVERYTHING GOOD AND BAD STARTS BECAUSE SOMEBODY DOES SOMETHING OR DOES NOT DO SOMETHING."
—SYLVIA EARLE, MARINE BIOLOGIST, EXPLORER, AND AQUANAUT

IF YOU COULD FIX ONE OF THE WORLD'S BIG
PROBLEMS, WHICH ONE WOULD YOU FIX AND WHY?

"IF YOU LOVE SCIENCE, ALL YOU
REALLY WANT IS TO KEEP WORKING."
—MARIA GOEPPERT-MAYER, NOBEL PRIZE—WINNING
THEORETICAL PHYSICIST

DETAILED OBSERVATIONS

DRAW A DIAGRAM TO EXPLAIN SOMETHING
THAT YOU LEARNED RECENTLY.

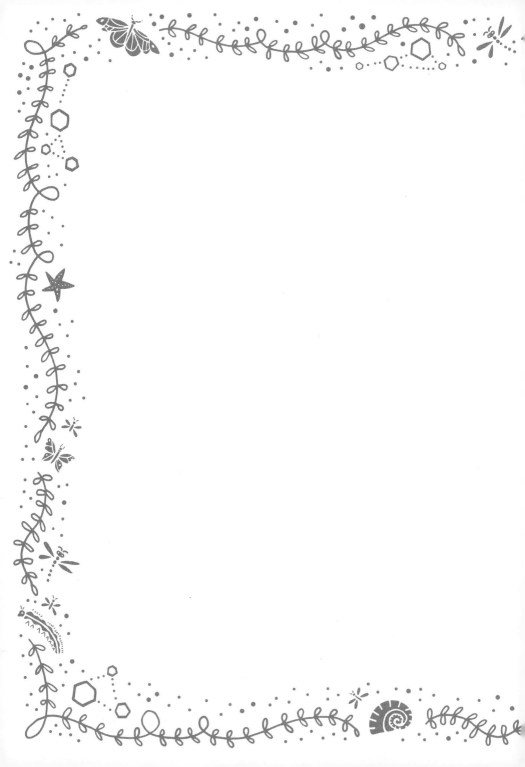

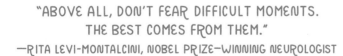

"ABOVE ALL, DON'T FEAR DIFFICULT MOMENTS.
THE BEST COMES FROM THEM."
—RITA LEVI-MONTALCINI, NOBEL PRIZE–WINNING NEUROLOGIST

NAME THREE FEARS THAT YOU HAVE. IS THERE ANYTHING YOU CAN DO TO HELP YOU OVERCOME YOUR FEARS?

"DON'T BE ARROGANT, BECAUSE ARROGANCE KILLS CURIOSITY."
—MINA BISSELL, BIOLOGIST

NAME A TIME YOU WERE WRONG OR FAILED TO
ACHIEVE YOUR GOAL. WHAT DID YOU LEARN FROM IT?

"WE MUST BELIEVE
IN OURSELVES
OR NO ONE
ELSE WILL
BELIEVE IN US;
WE MUST MATCH OUR
ASPIRATIONS WITH
THE COMPETENCE,
COURAGE, AND
DETERMINATION
TO SUCCEED."

—ROSALYN YALOW,
NOBEL PRIZE—WINNING
MEDICAL PHYSICIST

NAME THREE PEOPLE IN YOUR LIFE WHO GIVE YOU STRENGTH. HOW DO THEY ENCOURAGE YOU?

"HOPE AND CURIOSITY ABOUT THE FUTURE SEEMED
BETTER [TO ME] THAN GUARANTEES."
—HEDY LAMARR, INVENTOR AND ACTOR

DO YOU REMEMBER YOUR DREAMS?
WHAT DO YOU USUALLY DREAM ABOUT?

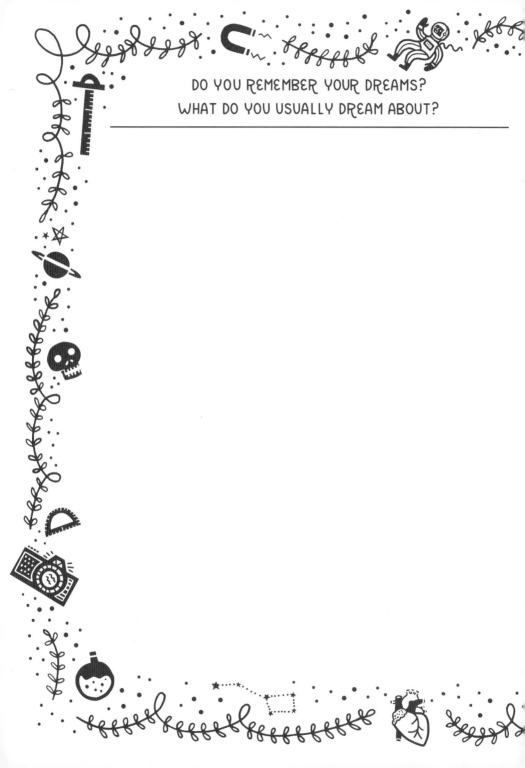

"SAY WHAT YOU KNOW, DO WHAT
YOU MUST, COME WHAT MAY."
—SOFIA KOVALEVSKAYA, MATHEMATICIAN

GO OUTSIDE AND LOOK FOR CONSTELLATIONS
IN THE NIGHT SKY. DRAW WHAT YOU SEE.

DETAILED OBSERVATIONS

"WE HUMANS, THOUGH TROUBLED AND WARLIKE,
ARE ALSO THE DREAMERS, THINKERS, AND EXPLORERS
INHABITING ONE ACHINGLY BEAUTIFUL PLANET, YEARNING
FOR THE SUBLIME, AND CAPABLE OF THE MAGNIFICENT."
—CAROLYN PORCO, PLANETARY SCIENTIST

WHAT EXPERIENCES IN YOUR LIFE HAVE INSPIRED YOUR PASSION FOR SCIENCE AND LEARNING?

WHAT IN NATURE DO YOU FIND MOST FASCINATING?

"THOSE WHO DWELL AMONG THE BEAUTIES AND MYSTERIES OF THE EARTH ARE NEVER ALONE OR WEARY OF LIFE."

—RACHEL CARSON, MARINE BIOLOGIST, CONSERVATIONIST, AND AUTHOR

NINETY-FIVE PERCENT OF EARTH'S OCEANS ARE
STILL UNEXPLORED—THERE IS STILL SO MUCH
THAT WE DON'T KNOW ABOUT OUR WORLD.
WHAT DO YOU WANT TO DISCOVER?

"FIRST OF ALL, YOU HAVE TO LOVE [WHAT YOU DO],
BECAUSE IF THERE IS ANY OTHER REASON FOR GOING INTO
IT, IT WON'T WORK. SECONDLY, YOU HAVE TO BE YOURSELF.
YOU HAVE TO RECOGNIZE YOUR UNIQUE CHARACTERISTICS
AND WHAT YOUR TALENTS ARE."

—EDITH FLANIGEN, CHEMIST

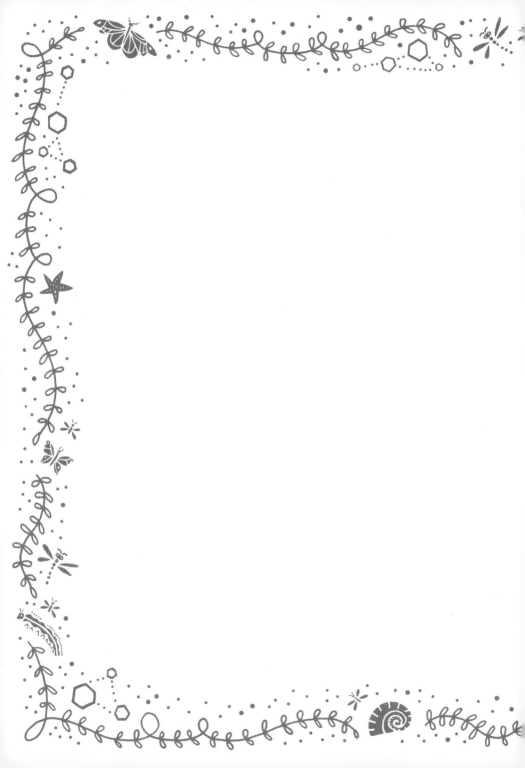

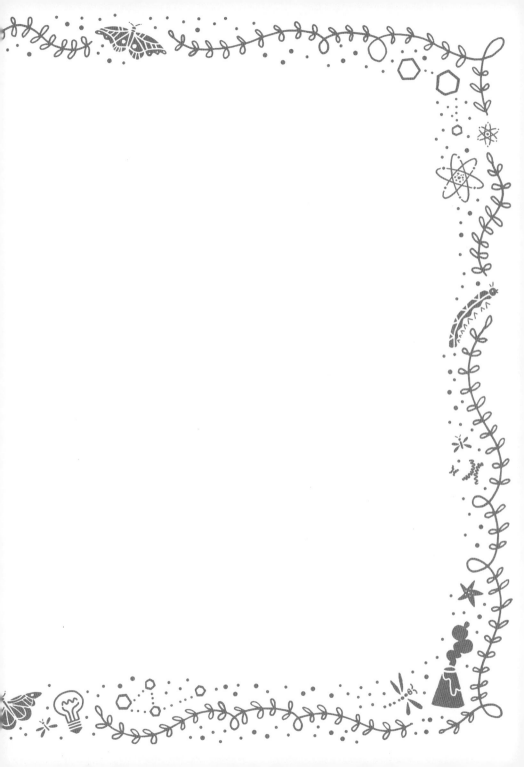

WHO IN YOUR LIFE PUSHES YOU TO GROW?
WHO ENCOURAGES YOU TO FOLLOW YOUR DREAMS?

"IT IS INVALUABLE TO HAVE A FRIEND WHO SHARES YOUR
INTERESTS AND HELPS YOU STAY MOTIVATED."
—MARYAM MIRZAKHANI, MATHEMATICIAN

WRITE DOWN TEN OF YOUR BIG LIFE GOALS.

1.

2.

3.

4.

5.

6.

7.

8.

9.

10.

"THE MOST DAMAGING PHRASE IN THE LANGUAGE IS,
'WE'VE ALWAYS DONE IT THIS WAY!'"
—GRACE HOPPER, COMPUTER SCIENTIST AND NAVY ADMIRAL

WHEN AND WHERE DO YOU GET YOUR BEST IDEAS?

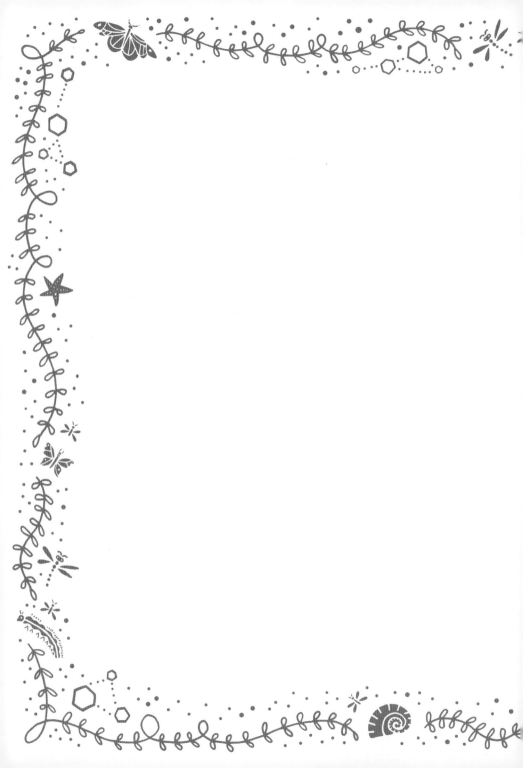

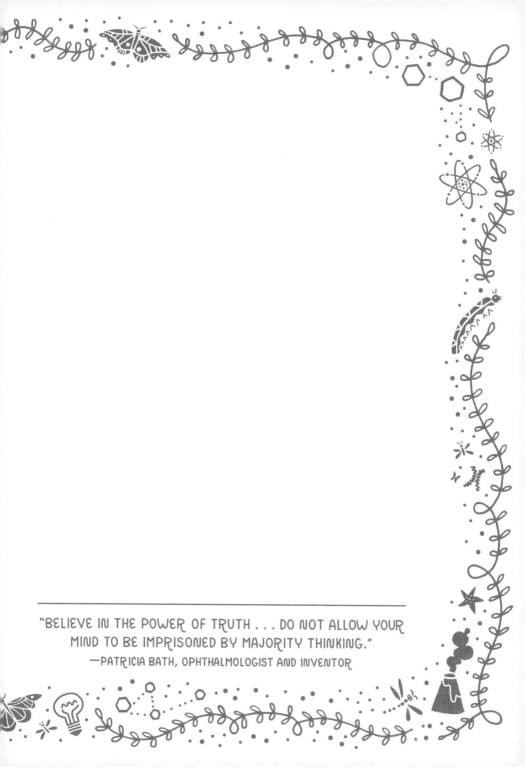

"BELIEVE IN THE POWER OF TRUTH . . . DO NOT ALLOW YOUR
MIND TO BE IMPRISONED BY MAJORITY THINKING."
—PATRICIA BATH, OPHTHALMOLOGIST AND INVENTOR

"I WOULD LIKE TO BE REMEMBERED AS SOMEONE
WHO WAS NOT AFRAID TO DO WHAT SHE WANTED
TO DO, AND AS SOMEONE WHO TOOK RISKS ALONG
THE WAY IN ORDER TO ACHIEVE HER GOALS."
—SALLY RIDE, ASTRONAUT AND FIRST AMERICAN WOMAN IN SPACE

IF YOU COULD TAKE THREE ITEMS WITH
YOU INTO SPACE, WHAT WOULD THEY BE?

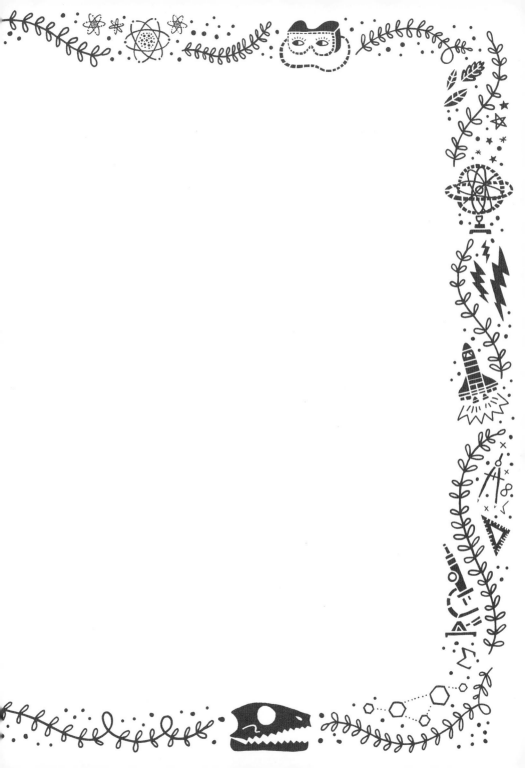

"WE ACCEPTED EDUCATION AS THE MEANS TO RISE
ABOVE THE LIMITATIONS THAT A PREJUDICED SOCIETY
ENDEAVORED TO PLACE UPON US."
—EVELYN BOYD GRANVILLE, MATHEMATICIAN AND DEVELOPER FOR IBM

WHAT IS YOUR FAVORITE SUBJECT TO STUDY AND WHY?

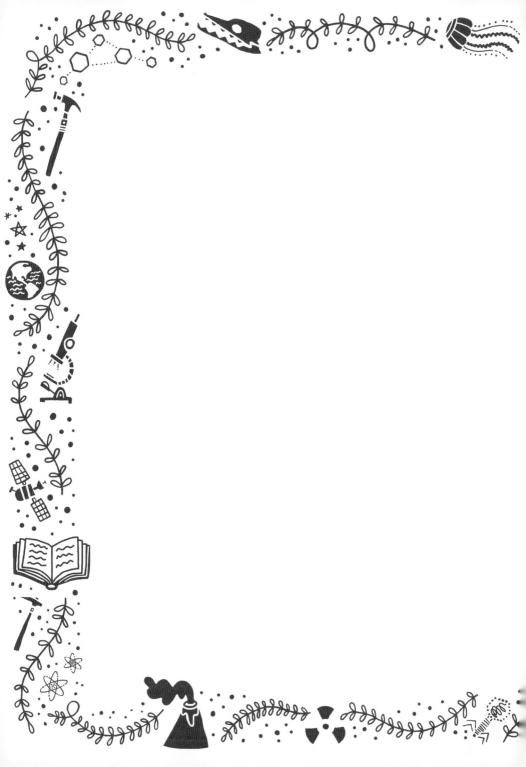

"YOU DON'T WANT TO JUST DO A PROBLEM BECAUSE IT'S EASY TO SOLVE, YOU WANT TO DO SOMETHING THAT YOU'RE OBSESSED WITH, THAT YOU JUST HAVE TO UNDERSTAND, BECAUSE THAT'S WHERE THE JOY COMES FROM."
—LINDA BUCK, NOBEL PRIZE–WINNING BIOLOGIST

WHO ARE YOUR HEROES?
WHAT ABOUT THEM DO YOU ADMIRE THE MOST?

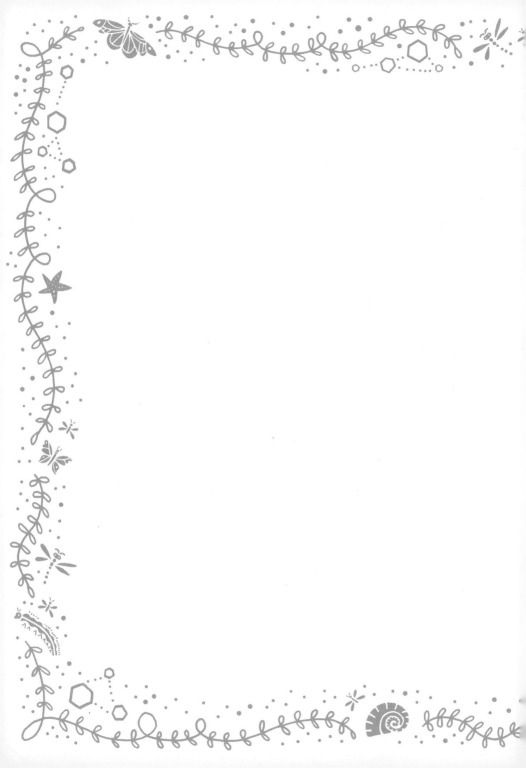

ONLY ABOUT 10 PERCENT OF AN ICEBERG CAN
BE SEEN ABOVE THE SURFACE OF THE WATER—
THE OTHER 90 PERCENT IS HIDDEN BELOW. WHAT
ABOUT YOU ISN'T EASY TO SEE ON THE SURFACE?

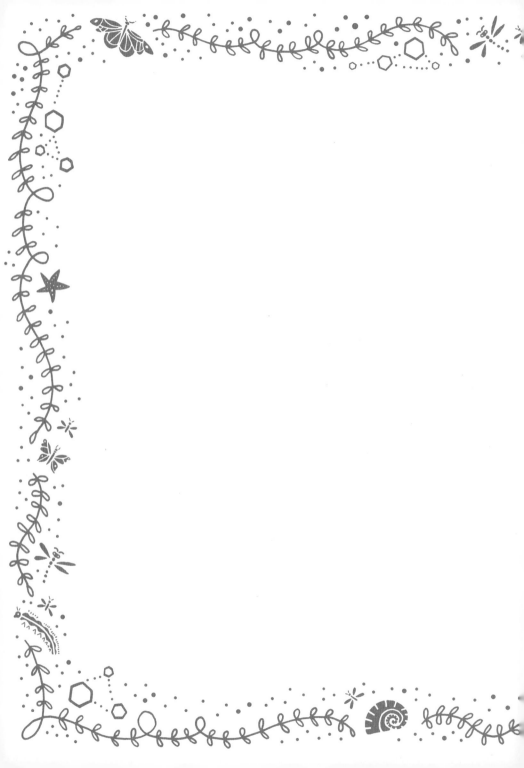

"SCIENCE DOESN'T ALWAYS GO FORWARDS.
IT'S A BIT LIKE DOING A RUBIK'S CUBE. YOU
SOMETIMES HAVE TO MAKE MORE OF A MESS WITH
A RUBIK'S CUBE BEFORE YOU CAN GET IT TO GO RIGHT."
—JOCELYN BELL BURNELL, ASTROPHYSICIST

GO SOMEPLACE YOU HAVE NEVER
BEEN AND DRAW WHAT YOU SEE.

DETAILED OBSERVATIONS

WHEN YOU FEEL LIKE YOU WANT TO GIVE UP,
WHAT MOTIVATES YOU TO KEEP GOING?

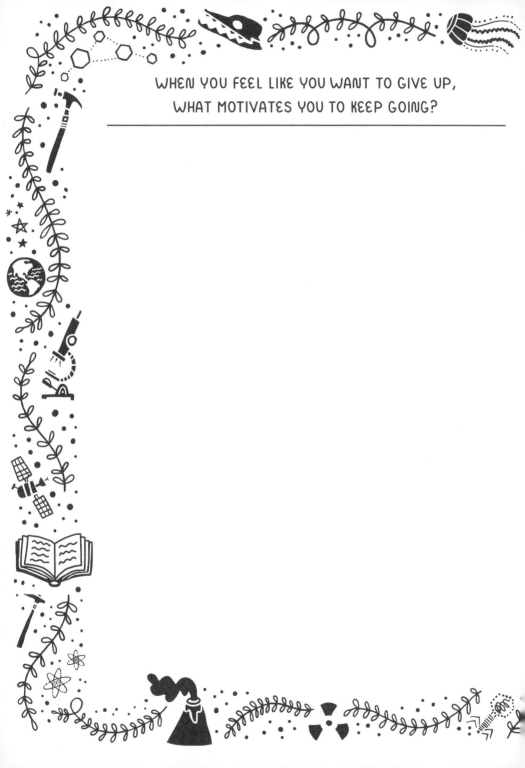

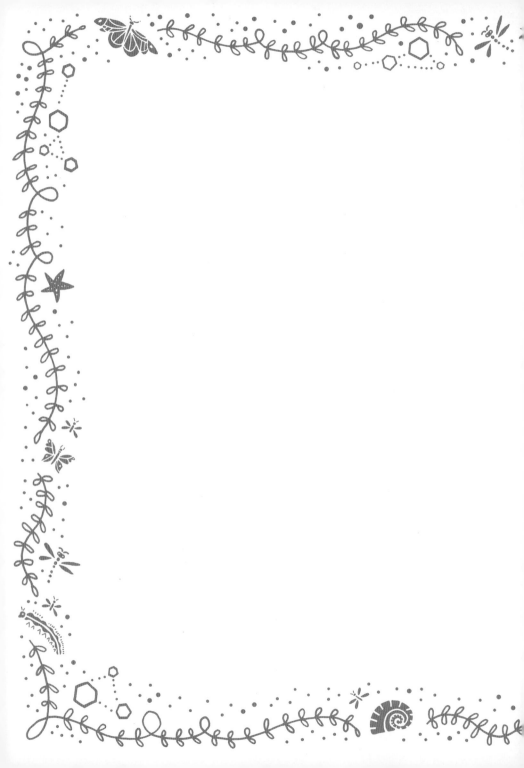

"LIFE NEED NOT BE EASY, PROVIDED ONLY THAT IT IS NOT EMPTY."
—LISE MEITNER, PHYSICIST

WHAT ARE THREE THINGS YOU CANNOT LIVE WITHOUT?
WHY ARE THESE THINGS IMPORTANT TO YOU?

"ONLY WHEN OUR CLEVER BRAIN AND OUR HUMAN HEART WORK TOGETHER IN HARMONY CAN WE ACHIEVE OUR FULL POTENTIAL."

—JANE GOODALL, PRIMATOLOGIST, ETHNOLOGIST, AND ANTHROPOLOGIST

WHAT ARE YOUR FAVORITE BOOKS?
WHAT DO YOU LOVE ABOUT THEM?

"IF YOU KNOW YOU ARE ON THE RIGHT TRACK, IF YOU HAVE THIS INNER KNOWLEDGE, THEN NOBODY CAN TURN YOU OFF.... NO MATTER WHAT THEY SAY."
—BARBARA MCCLINTOCK, NOBEL PRIZE—WINNING CYTOGENETICIST

IF YOU COULD TRAVEL ANYWHERE IN THE UNIVERSE, WHERE WOULD IT BE AND WHY? WHAT WOULD YOU WANT TO SEE?

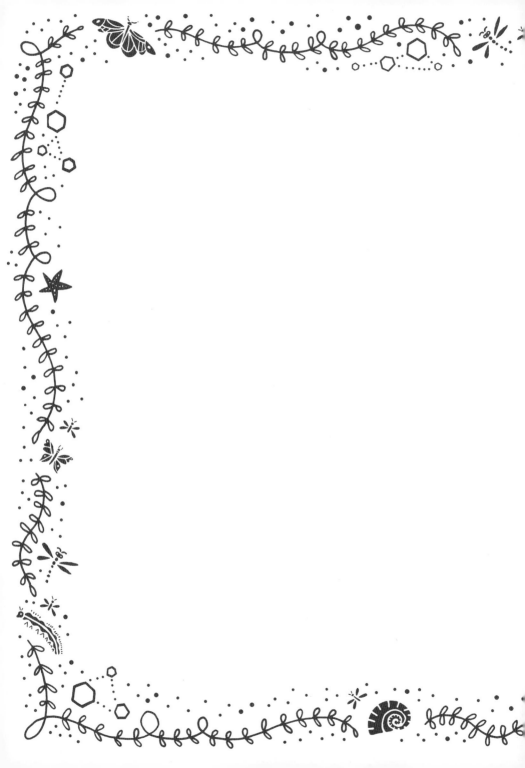

"ALL OF US HAVE TALENTS AND HAVE THINGS TO CONTRIBUTE . . .
NEVER LET OTHERS DEFINE WHAT YOUR LIFE CAN BE."
—SHIRLEY ANN JACKSON, PHYSICIST

WHAT QUALITIES IN YOURSELF ARE YOU MOST PROUD OF?

ALL RIGHTS RESERVED.
PUBLISHED IN THE UNITED STATES BY TEN SPEED PRESS,
AN IMPRINT OF THE CROWN PUBLISHING GROUP,
A DIVISION OF PENGUIN RANDOM HOUSE LLC, NEW YORK.
WWW.CROWNPUBLISHING.COM
WWW.TENSPEED.COM

TEN SPEED PRESS AND THE TEN SPEED PRESS COLOPHON ARE
REGISTERED TRADEMARKS OF PENGUIN RANDOM HOUSE LLC.

BASED ON THE BOOK WOMEN IN SCIENCE BY RACHEL IGNOTOFSKY,
PUBLISHED BY TEN SPEED PRESS, BERKELEY, IN 2016.

LIBRARY OF CONGRESS CATALOGING-IN-PUBLICATION DATA
NAMES: IGNOTOFSKY, RACHEL, 1989-
TITLE: I LOVE SCIENCE : A JOURNAL FOR SELF-DISCOVERY AND
   BIG IDEAS / BY RACHEL IGNOTOFSKY.
DESCRIPTION: BERKELEY : TEN SPEED PRESS, [2017] I INCLUDES
   BIBLIOGRAPHICAL REFERENCES AND INDEX.
IDENTIFIERS: LCCN 2016038157 I ISBN 9781607749806 (TRADE PBK. : ALK. PAPER)
SUBJECTS: LCSH: WOMEN IN SCIENCE—JUVENILE LITERATURE. I WOMEN
   SCIENTISTS—JUVENILE LITERATURE. I SCIENCE—QUOTATIONS, MAXIMS,
   ETC. I GIRLS—EDUCATION. I YOUNG WOMEN—EDUCATION.
CLASSIFICATION: LCC Q130 .I36 2017 I DDC 500—DC23 LC RECORD AVAILABLE
   AT HTTPS://LCCN.LOC.GOV/2016038157

TRADE PAPERBACK ISBN: 978-1-60774-980-6

PRINTED IN CHINA

DESIGN BY ANGELINA CHENEY

10 9 8 7 6 5 4 3 2 1

FIRST EDITION